The LAZY GIANT

Ivan Jones

Illustrated by
Dee Shulman

OXFORD
UNIVERSITY PRESS

UNIVERSITY PRESS

Great Clarendon Street, Oxford, OX2 6DP,
United Kingdom

Oxford University Press is a department of the University of Oxford.
It furthers the University's objective of excellence in research, scholarship,
and education by publishing worldwide. Oxford is a registered trade mark of
Oxford University Press in the UK and in certain other countries

Text © Ivan Jones 2003

The moral rights of the author have been asserted

First published in this edition 2016

All rights reserved. No part of this publication may be reproduced, stored
in a retrieval system, or transmitted, in any form or by any means, without
the prior permission in writing of Oxford University Press, or as expressly
permitted by law, by licence or under terms agreed with the appropriate
reprographics rights organization. Enquiries concerning reproduction outside
the scope of the above should be sent to the Rights Department, Oxford
University Press, at the address above.

You must not circulate this work in any other form
and you must impose this same condition on any acquirer

British Library Cataloguing in Publication Data
Data available

978-0-19-837707-8

3 5 7 9 10 8 6 4 2

Paper used in the production of this book is a natural, recyclable product
made from wood grown in sustainable forests. The manufacturing process
conforms to the environmental regulations of the country of origin.

Printed in China by Leo Paper Products Ltd.

Acknowledgements
Cover and inside illustrations by Dee Shulman
Inside cover notes written by Gill Howell

Contents

1	The Giant	5
2	"Is My Breakfast Ready?"	8
3	"Is My Castle Clean?"	12
4	"Hurry Up!"	20
5	Just in Time	27
	About the author	32

Chapter 1

The Giant

Once there was a horrible old Giant. He lived in a big castle on top of a mountain, and he was very lazy.

The Giant was so lazy, he needed servants to look after him.

But nobody wanted to work for him at all.

One day, the Giant went down the mountain. At the bottom there was a little cottage. Twelve children lived there, all on their own.

The girls were called:

Lotty, Dotty and Totty,

and Bessie, Jessie and Nessie.

And the boys were called:

Cliff, Riff and Sniff,

and Ken, Ben and Den.

"Now they would make good servants," thought the Giant. So he carried them off, back to his castle.

Chapter 2

"Is My Breakfast Ready?"

Every morning, the children had to get up very early, light the big fire and fetch lots of water. Then they had to make a huge pot of porridge for the Giant.

At six o'clock, the Giant would yell,

But one morning, the children woke up a bit late.

The fire wouldn't light and the water wouldn't flow. So the Giant's porridge was lumpy.

"YOU LAZY LOT!" roared the Giant.
All the children started to shake,
The castle itself began to quake!

The Giant was so angry, he picked up Totty and dropped her into his bowl of porridge.

Now Totty was the smallest child of all.
She was only as tall as the Giant's boot.
Her little yellow hat fell off and bobbed
on top of the porridge.

"Yuk! Yuk! Yuk!" cried Totty.

"I may be teeny,

But I do not scream,

Not even for a giant so mean!"

As soon as the Giant's back was turned,
Lotty and Dotty pulled Totty out. Without
her hat, she looked smaller than ever.

Chapter 3

"Is My Castle Clean?"

Every afternoon the children had to
polish and rub, sweep and scrub.
And everything had to shine
like a new pin.

At two o'clock, the Giant would yell,

But one afternoon, the polish ran out.

The head fell off the broom and the bristles fell out of the huge scrubbing brush.

And the Giant found some cobwebs in a corner.

"YOU DIRTY DUCKS!" boomed the Giant.

All the children started to shake,
The castle itself began to quake!

The Giant was so angry that he picked up Nessie and dropped her into the waste basket.

Now Nessie was the untidiest of all the children. She always left things on the floor and forgot to comb her hair.

"Ugh!" she cried. "I'm in a stew!

There's rubbish all over me,

What can I do?"

Just as soon as the Giant's back was turned, Bessie and Jessie pulled Nessie out.

Poor Nessie! She looked untidier than ever!

Every night, the children had to warm the Giant's bed with a big hot water bottle. And the sheets had to be clean and smooth.

At ten o'clock, the
Giant would growl,

But one night, the hot water bottle
had a hole in it. Water ran on to the bed.
And the Giant found the sheets were cold
and damp.

"YOU SICKENING SNAILS!" roared the Giant.

All the children started to shake,
The castle itself began to quake!

The Giant was so angry that he picked up Sniff and dropped him in the sink. It was huge!

Now Sniff always had a cold. But he never moaned. He was always cheerful.

"Help!" he cried.

"This sink's like an ocean!

It has a very choppy motion.

The water's rough and dirty brown.
Get me out, before I drown!"

As soon as the
Giant's back was
turned, Riff and Cliff
fished out Sniff.
After his swim in
the Giant's
sink, Sniff
sniffed
worse
than ever.

Chapter 4

"Hurry Up!"

Every Sunday, the children had to get the Giant's carriage ready. They had to pull it up and down the mountain.

He would lie on soft cushions inside it.

At eleven o'clock, the Giant would roar, "WHERE IS MY CARRIAGE?"

But one Sunday, it rained and rained. The lane was muddy and the wheels were wobbly. And so the Giant wasn't going as fast as he liked. He roared.

*All the children
started to shake,
The carriage itself
began to quake!*

The Giant was so
angry that he reached
out of the carriage
and gave Den
a push.

Now Den was the strongest of all the children. He rolled and rolled until he was out of sight.

When the other children saw what the Giant had done, they were very upset. But they pulled the carriage to the top of the mountain.

They all nodded.

The children gave the carriage a huge PUSH!!!

The carriage raced down the hill.
It creaked and rattled.
It banged and
clattered.

The Giant bounced out of the carriage! He rolled down the mountain until …

He fell into a muddy hole.

Chapter 5

Just in Time

The Giant was very angry.
"YOU NINCOMPOOPS!" he roared.

GET ME OUT!

But the children were safely out of the Giant's reach.

And then Ken and Ben heard a voice.

"Help!" it said.
"Den I was and Den I am.
I thought I'd never see you again.
But thanks to the tree on the side of the hill, your strongest friend is with you still!"

Den was hanging on a tree branch.

As quickly as they could, the children rescued him. They were just in time!

GET ME OUT OF HERE!

The Giant was bellowing and banging, yelling and thumping. He made so much noise, the rocks on the mountain began to tumble.

Before the Giant could say, "YOU TERRIBLE TOADS!", a big rock rolled down the mountain and clonked him on the head. He was knocked out cold!

Quick as a wink, the children ran down the mountainside, laughing and shouting. They were so happy to go back home again.

As for the Giant, he got himself out of the hole and crawled back to his castle.

He never tried to catch the children again. And so, if ever he wanted anything done, he had to do it – himself!

About the author

When I was growing up, I was told legends about giants. I also read *Jack the Giant Killer* stories. Later on, I read Oscar Wilde's wonderful tale, *The Selfish Giant.* I thought I'd like to write my own giant stories. I wanted them to be funny and scary, and I wanted them to say something – a sort of message.